BEYOND THE HORIZON

Overcoming the Fear of Death

CHARLES G. BRANZ

Love is immortal; life is eternal, and death is merely a horizon; and a horizon is nothing save the limit of our sight...

—AUTHOR UNKNOWN

DEDICATION

I am proud to dedicate the new edition of this book to Carol, my first wife of forty-seven years. She is now residing "Beyond the Horizon" with her Savior and Lord.

CONTENTS

"And also that He (Jesus Christ) might deliver and completely set free all those who, through the [haunting] fear of death, were held in bondage throughout the whole course of their lives."1

—HEBREWS 2:15

"For God has not given us the spirit of fear; but of power and of love and of a sound mind."

—II TIMOTHY 1:7

DID YOU KNOW THAT...

The body is wonderfully made? (Psalm 139:14). It consists of various chemicals worth about 98 cents. The body has 263 bones, 600 muscles, 970 miles of blood vessels, 400 cups on the tongue for taste, 20,000 hairs in the ears to tune in to all sound; 40 pounds of jaw pressure, 10,000,000 nerves and branches, 3,500 sweat tubes to each square inch of skin adding up to 40 miles in length, 600,000,000 air cells in the lungs that inhale 2,400 gallons of air daily, and a telephone system that relates to the brain instantly any known sound, taste, sight, touch or smell. The heart beats 4,200 times an hour and pumps 12 tons of blood daily.[2]

PREFACE

HAVING BEEN IN THE MEDICAL profession for forty-nine years, as well as being a minister of the Gospel of Jesus Christ, I have seen too often how the fear of death and the uncertainty of where we are to go after physical death ravage people's lives. I have read many books on how to deal with death in a worldly sense. Many of them are beautiful, poetic, and temporarily soothing to the mind. However, my desire in this book is to help you develop an understanding and a sure foundation for life after death according to the Word of God.

It is my intention to give scriptural evidence and assurance of the fact that death, departing from earth, need never be something that causes fear or foreboding, but rather joy and peace in the sure knowledge of our final destination, to those who have made Jesus Christ their personal Savior. Yes, there is a hell to avoid, but in Christ we have been given the keys to death and the grave. Our future holds the glorious promise of eternity with our Father in heaven.

When you finish reading this book, there should be no doubt in your mind as to where you are going when departing this life—you should have no fear and no anxiety! Heb. 2:14-15 says,

"Since, therefore, [these His] children share in the flesh and blood [in the physical nature of human beings], He [Himself] in a similar manner partook of the same [nature], that by [going through] death He might bring to naught and make of no effect him who had the power of death—that is, the devil—And also that He might deliver and completely set free all those who through the [haunting] fear of death were held in bondage throughout the whole course of their lives."[1]

We have God's own word of assurance—*We need not fear death!* I believe every person in the Kingdom of God should have a copy of this book, not only for themselves, but as an aid in ministering salvation to all those who are unbelievers.

ACKNOWLEDGEMENTS

It is impossible to write a book without the help from those with writing and artistic skills, of which I have neither. I want to thank my wife Susan for the countless hours of re-editing the previous book, and for her artistic skills for the photograph and design of the book cover.

I also want to thank Michelle Mason, director of Insight International, for her patience and input with developing this edition.

INTRODUCTION

THE PURPOSE OF THIS BOOK is twofold: first to show you according to the Bible that God is not the author of death, and second that you have nothing to fear in death if you have made Jesus Christ your personal Lord and Savior. *This book will not attempt to discuss the emotional aspects of death, the handling of grief, or the doctrinal theologies of death.* I desire only to simplify the scriptural definition of death and the effects of death, in order that you may have an understanding which will once and for all dispel any doubts and fears concerning it. It should also make a good tool to use when ministering to those who may have a terminal illness.

I believe that the greatest fear known to mankind is the fear of death. The vast majority of people are probably not able to discuss death reasonably and calmly. As a matter of fact, most people will avoid any discussion of death because of their deep-seated fear of the unknown. They rationalize that if they don't talk about it, it will eventually go away and they won't have to deal with it.

It is not the intent of the author to force any religious views upon anyone—the contents are God's Word on the subject of death and you can believe it or reject it. No one, including God Himself, will ever force you to believe in His Word. God's Word contains spiritual laws—which never vary or change, and remain consistent every time, exactly the same as natural laws.

For example, consider the law of gravity. If you drop a pencil to the floor one hundred times, it will fall to the floor one hundred times unless a different law comes into effect. You may choose not to believe in gravity, but I can guarantee you that if you step off the roof of a building, you will surely fall to the ground. Your believing or not believing a physical or spiritual law will never change it.

God is not the author of death but is the author of life. He created man to fellowship with Him and to live with Him forever. He desires to have all mankind call upon Him as their heavenly Father who is love, and upon His Son Jesus who is the expression of that love. *Jesus is the revelation of the will of God for all mankind for all time.* At this very moment Jesus is in heaven with a flesh and bone body—immortal and eternal. We who have received Jesus as our Savior will someday have a glorified body as His, one in which we will be able to sit down and eat a solid meal, and also be able to walk through a wall (Mark 16:12,14; Luke 24:36; John 20:19 & 21:12-14).

My desire is to show you, according to the Bible, that you never need to fear death; you can overcome the fear that is associated with the idea of death. God is a God of faith and faith is the exact opposite or reciprocal of fear.

The devil (and there is a devil) has taken everything that God created for good and has perverted it—I.E., love to hate, prosperity to poverty, good health to sickness and disease, and life unto death!

However, God has good news for you. John 3:16, *"For God so greatly loved and dearly prized the world that He [even] gave up His only begotten (unique) Son, so that whoever believes in (trusts in, clings to, relies on) Him shall not perish (come to destruction, be lost) but have eternal (everlasting) life."*1 Jesus said in John 11:25-26, *"I am the resurrection and the life. He who believes in me, though he may die, he shall live. And whoever lives and believes in Me shall never die. Do you believe this?"*

What did Jesus mean by we shall never die? I want you to clear your mind of whatever you may have been taught or any preconceived ideas you might have concerning death and let the Spirit of God lead you to the truth as you read through to the end of this book.

Chapter 1

DEFINITIONS

DEATH: The word *death*, as applied to man in the scriptures, means a separation or cutting away from. The word *separation* can be logically substituted for the word *death* in every instance without violating the integrity of the scriptures. It helps to clarify many passages to do so, as we shall see. On the other hand, the word *death* NEVER means the annihilation or extinction of being or the cessation of life.2,3

PHYSICAL DEATH is the separation of the inner man, the soul and spirit, from the outer man, the body. James 2:26, *"For as the body without the spirit is dead..."* The body only dies at this time and goes back to dust. Gen. 3:19,*"...till you return to the ground, for out of it you were taken; for dust you are, and to dust you shalt return."* It does not say the spirit without the body shall return to dust, but the body without the spirit!

SPIRITUAL DEATH is the separation of man from God due to sin, the cutting away from the realization of the purpose for which God created him. One who is spiritually dead can be alive physically. I Tim. 5:6, *"But she who lives in pleasure is dead while she lives."*

Matt. 8:22, *"But Jesus said to him, Follow me, and let the dead bury their own dead."* These two scriptures point out that one can be physically alive but spiritually dead.

ETERNAL is used of persons and things which are, in their nature, without end or forever.3

MORTAL means subject or liable to death. The body is called mortal not simply because it is liable to death, but because it is the organ in and through which death carries on its death-producing activities. Mortal is applied to the flesh, which consists of the element of decay, and is thereby death-doomed.2,3

IMMORTAL literally means the deathlessness of the glorified body of the believer—as the now-resurrected body of Jesus Christ—a flesh and bone body which is also eternal.2,3

ETERNAL DEATH or "the second death" means eternal separation from God as a result of his (man's) own choice. When man chooses to reject Jesus and remain in sin he will spend eternity separated from God in the Lake of Fire. Rev. 2:11, *"...He who overcomes shall not be hurt by the second death."* Rev. 20:6, *"Blessed and holy is he who has part in the first resurrection. Over such the second death has no power, but they shall be priests of God and of Christ, and shall reign with Him a thousand years,"* and vs. 14, *"Then death and Hades were cast into the Lake of Fire. This is the second death."*2,3

Chapter 2

SPIRIT, SOUL, & BODY

THE SPECIES OF MAN is a three-part living being. We are a spirit—made in the image and likeness of God (Gen. 1:26-27; Gen. 9:6; Col. 3:10; James 3:9,27); we have a soul; and we live in a body. I Thess. 5:23, *"...may your whole spirit, soul, and body be preserved blameless at the coming of our Lord Jesus Christ."* Heb. 4:12, *"For the Word of God is living and powerful, and sharper than any two-edged sword, piercing even to the division of soul and spirit, and of joints and marrow, and is a discerner of the thoughts and intents of the heart."* In this verse joints and marrow refer to the body. Luke 1:46-47, *"And Mary said: My soul magnifies the Lord, and my spirit has rejoiced in God my Savior."*

The common understanding has been that man is comprised of a body which has a soul, the emphasis being on the body. But as you can see, the scriptures point out that we are a spirit first, which has a soul (made of the mind, will, intellect, and emotions) and we live in a body!

THE BODY (TABERNACLE, TENT)

The Apostle Peter referred to his body as a tabernacle (tent) in II Peter 1:13-14. *"Yes, I think it is right, as long as I am in this tent, to stir you up by reminding you, knowing that shortly I must put off my tent, even as our Lord Jesus Christ showed me."*

The Apostle Paul also called his body a tabernacle or tent. II Cor. 5:1,4, *"For we know that if the tent which is our earthly home is destroyed (dissolved), we have from God a building, a house not made with hands, eternal in the heavens." "For while we are still in this tent, we groan under the burden and sigh deeply (weighed down, depressed, oppressed)—not that we want to put off the body (the clothing of the spirit), but rather that we would be further clothed so that what is mortal (our dying body) may be swallowed up by life [after the resurrection]."*[1]

Look at what the above scripture said about our body being the clothing of the real man-the spirit! I like to think of this body being like a space suit and my spirit, which is the real me, is housed inside that suit, looking out through two windows (eyes). My body is only a vehicle, as is a space suit, to enable the real me (spirit) to deal with the natural earth around me.

In the same way that only our spirits communicate with God, we have natural bodies and senses which enable us to deal with the natural realm.

THE SPIRIT (INNER OR INWARD MAN)

The Apostle Paul talks about our spirits being the inner or inward man. Eph. 3:16, *"May He grant you out of the rich treasury of His glory to be strengthened and reinforced with mighty power in the inner man by the [Holy] Spirit [Himself indwelling your innermost being and personality]."*1 Rom. 7:22, *"For I delight in the Law of God according to the inward man..."* II Cor. 4:16, *"Even though our outward man is perishing, yet the inward man is being renewed day by day."*

Paul goes on to say that while he (spirit) is in the body, he (spirit) is absent from the Lord. II Cor. 5:6,8, *"So then, we are always full of good and hopeful and confident courage; we know that while we are at home in the body, we are abroad from the home with the Lord [that is promised us]." "[Yes] we have confident and hopeful courage and are pleased rather to be away from home out of the body and be at home with the Lord."*1

Paul also talks about a heavenly experience in which he was given all the revelations of the scriptures which he records in his letters in the New Testament. II Cor. 12:2-4, *"I know a man in Christ who fourteen years ago—whether in the body or out of the body I do not know, God knows—was caught up to the third heaven. And I know that this man—whether in the body or away from the body I do not know, God knows—was caught up into paradise, and he heard utterances beyond the power of man to put into words, which man is not permitted to utter."*1

What Paul was saying is that the real man (the inward man) does not look any different than the outward man (the flesh) because in the spirit realm he could not tell the difference.

Because we live in a physical and natural world, it is difficult to realize that the spirit world is far more real than this natural world. We think of people as existing only in their physical bodies, and when they have died as no longer existing at all. Yet the Bible tells us that the *real* man is the inward man, the hidden man of the heart, and he is an eternal being. He *will* live on after his physical body has returned to dust.

So we have discovered that the species man has a three-fold nature:

1. Spirit: The dimension of man which deals with the spiritual realm—that part of man which knows God.

2. Soul: The dimension of man which deals with the mental realm, or man's intellect, sensibilities, emotions, and will—the part that reasons, thinks, and feels.

3. Body: That part of a man which deals with the physical realm—the house, tent, or tabernacle in which we live.

Having read what God says about us, we should begin thinking of ourselves in a new way. We are not just a physical being but a spirit being who possesses a soul and lives in a body!

Chapter 3

THE BODY

YOU ARE THE CARETAKER OF YOUR BODY

We ended the last chapter with the observation that we are a spirit, we have a soul, and we live in a body! In this chapter, we will discuss these three in reverse order, starting with the body, because this is where most people's awareness is centered.

The word for body in the Greek is *"soma"* and is used to connote the physical nature which is distinct and different from *"pneuma"*, the spiritual nature, and *"psuche"*, the soul. I Thess. 5:23, *"...and may your whole spirit, soul, and body be preserved blameless..."*

The Bible speaks of our bodies as being the outward man, a tent, a tabernacle, the physical house in which we (spirit) live. The Apostle Paul said in Rom. 12:1, writing to Christians and not to non-believers, *"I beseech you therefore, brethren, by the mercies of God, that you present your bodies a living sacrifice, holy, acceptable to God, which is your reasonable service."* He was not asking God to do something with our bodies, but rather exhorting us to do something with them—(YOU) *"present your bodies a living sacrifice."*

God has already done everything He needs to do for us through His Son Jesus Christ by way of His death, burial, and resurrection. It is up to us to do something with our bodies.

The scripture I just quoted said that we (the inward man) are to present our bodies (the house in which we live). In other words, we (the spirit man) are the care-takers of that house. Paul tells us that both the spirit man, whom we are, and the body (house) in which we live are indwelt by the Spirit of God and that, as such, both should be kept dwelling places of honor. I Cor. 3:16,17, *"Do you not know that you are the temple of God and that the Spirit of God dwells in you? If anyone defiles the temple of God, God will destroy him. For the temple of God is holy, which temple you are."*

This speaks of the inward man, the spirit. In I Cor. 6:19,20 the Spirit of God speaking through Paul said, *"Or do you not know that your body is the temple of the Holy Spirit who is in you, whom you have from God, and you are not your own? For you were bought at a price; therefore glorify God in your body and in your spirit, which are God's."*

The scripture goes on to say again that you (spirit) are to do something with your body. In I Cor. 9:27 Paul said, *"But I discipline my body, and bring it into subjection."* Who is the *I* about whom he is talking? *I am the man on the inside, the real ME!* If the body were the real you, Paul would have said, 'I keep myself under, I bring myself into subjection.' The *I* here is the eternal man, the man on inside, the hidden man of the heart, the real man.

DON'T BE FLESH RULED

You may now be asking, "Bring my body into subjection to what?" We are to bring our bodies into subjection to our inward man and not allow our bodies (our fleshly cravings and desires) to rule or dominate us. This is not mind control or the power of positive thinking, but rather acting on the power of God in your spirit man as your mind is renewed by the Word of God. That is why the Bible talks about carnality or flesh-ruled individuals.

Even Christians can be dominated or ruled by their bodily or fleshly desires rather than by their spirits. The Bible calls these people baby Christians—those who don't grow up spiritually in the things of God.

The Bible tells us that our bodies are corruptible or subject to decay (physical death), yet our inward man is renewed: *"though our outward man is [progressively] decaying and wasting away, yet our inner self is being [progressively] renewed day after day"* (II Cor. 4:16).[1] Even though our physical bodies are decaying or becoming older day by day, the Bible again tells us to take care of them in I Tim. 4:8. *"For physical training is of some value (useful for a little), but godliness (spiritual training) is useful and of value in everything and in every way, for it holds promise for the present life and also for the life which is to come."*[1] This scripture does not say that physical exercise does not profit at all but only a little. The emphasis should be on that which is spiritual because the body is subject to decay but the spirit is eternal.

Further evidence that the body is not the real man and that the spirit man can exist in and of himself, apart from the body is found in II Cor. 12:2,3, *"I know a man in Christ who fourteen years ago—whether in the body or out of the body I do not know, God knows—was caught up to the third heaven. And I know that this man— whether in the body or away from the body I do not know, God knows."*[1] What Paul is saying is that he (spirit) was taken up to heaven but he could not tell whether he was taken up physically or spiritually because he could not tell the difference between his physical body and his spiritual "body".

Although he could not tell the difference, he did surely know that there was a distinct difference. This suggests some possible answers to the questions concerning whether or not we will recognize others in the afterlife, but this will be discussed later.

The choice is ours. We can allow ourselves to be dominated or ruled over by our physical bodies and their desires, or we (the inward man) can choose to keep our bodies under control. Do we want our inward man to be able to present our bodies, a living sacrifice, to a loving and holy God? Again, the choice is ours!

THE BODY WILL RETURN TO DUST

At this point you may be asking, just what does happen to the body at the time of physical death? In Gen. 2:7 the scriptures tell us that the Lord God formed or molded man of the dust of the ground.

It is a scientific fact that the same essential chemical elements are found in man and animal bodies that are in the soil. The body is mortal, or subject to decay. It will decay eventually and go back to dust. Gen. 3:19, *"...until you return to the ground, for out of it you were taken; for dust you are, and to dust you shall return."* Eccl. 3:20, *"All go to one place; all are of the dust, and all turn to dust again."* Heb. 9:27, *"And as it is appointed for men to die once"* and James 2:26, *"For as the body without the spirit is dead..."*

All bodies do return to dust again, but nothing is said throughout scripture signifying that the souls and spirits, or the real invisible and intangible parts of men, were made of dust. The body is the only part of man that dies at physical death, and the reason it dies is because the inner man, the spirit of man, the life of the body leaves the body. The body then goes back to dust and is spoken of as being asleep. At some time in the future, the body will be resurrected in a glorified form just as Jesus was, and I will discuss that in a later chapter.

Chapter 4

THE SOUL

THE SOUL—THE MENTAL REALM

The word *soul* is generally distinguished from the body in phrases such as *body and soul* because we have traditionally been taught that the words soul and spirit have the same meaning. However, we give scriptural proof in the last chapter that there is a separation of spirit, soul, and body. I Thess. 5:23, *"...and may your spirit, and soul and body be preserved sound and complete..."* We see in Heb. 4:12 again that the Word of God distinguishes the soul from the spirit; *"For the Word of God is living and powerful, and sharper than any two-edged sword, piercing even to the division of soul and spirit, and of joints and morrow, and is a discerner of the thoughts and intents of the heart."*

Generally speaking, the spirit is the higher and the soul the lower element. The spirit may be recognized as the life principle bestowed on man by God, the soul as the resulting life constituted in the individual, the body being the material organism animated by soul and spirit.2

As was stated earlier, we can say that our soul consists of our mind (emotions, will, and intellect). The soulish realm of man is the part which thinks and reasons or, we might say the mental realm. The soul of man possesses appetites, exercises mental faculties, feelings, emotions, desires and passions. That is why we speak of the soul which feels and the spirit of man which knows.

The Apostle Paul said in Rom. 12:2, writing to Christians and not to non-believers, *"Do not be conformed to this world (this age), [fashioned after and adapted to its external, superficial customs], but be transformed (changed) by the [entire] renewal of your mind [by its new ideals and its new attitude], so that you may prove [for yourselves] what is the good and acceptable and perfect will of God, even the thing which is good and acceptable and perfect [in His sight for you]."*1 Paul was saying that we have to do something with our minds because God is not going to do anything with them, or with our bodies for that matter, because the first verse of the same chapter tells that we should present our bodies a living sacrifice.

DEVELOPING OUR SOULS

So we can either develop our soulish realm in the things that God has for us by renewing our minds to

His Word (scripture), or by what the world teaches which is ungodly. Our minds, as our bodies, can be fed "junk food" of this world (age) or they can feed on the "bread of life" which God provides through His Holy Word.

We also can exercise our intellect with man's wisdom, which is foolishness to God, or we can learn of God's wisdom which leads to the fullness of life. In the following verses, the Apostle Paul is talking to Christians and not the heathen in I Cor. 2:14,16. *"But the natural, nonspiritual man does not accept or welcome or admit into his heart the gifts and teachings and revelations of the Spirit of God, for they are folly (meaningless nonsense) to him; and he is incapable of knowing them...."* *"For who has known or understood the mind (counsels and purposes) of the Lord so as to guide and instruct Him and give Him knowledge? But we have the mind of Christ (the Messiah) and do hold the thoughts (feelings, and purposes) of His heart."*[1]

RENEWING OF OUR MINDS—PROCESS

We find that the greatest need in the church is the renewing of the minds of the people with the Word of God. Just because we are Christians does not necessarily mean that we have a renewed mind. It is imperative that our minds be fed on the Word of God, not humanism, psychology, sociology, or someone else's ideas of what the Word of God says.

Our minds become renewed only as we seek and search and study the scriptures for ourselves, combined with good teaching of the Word. This is a process which must continue on a daily basis. It has been said that we as Christians will eat three hot meals a day, seven days a week to nourish our bodies, and yet we feed our spirits only one cold snack a week (Sunday morning church)! In other words, our souls (minds) can and will only be renewed by daily feeding upon the Word of God by our own time spent in study and meditation.

Chapter 5

THE SPIRIT

THE SPIRIT—THE REAL MAN

The first and most important dimension of man is the spirit because the spirit man is the real man. As we stated earlier, man is a spirit who possesses a soul and lives in a body. It is the spirit of man that knows or makes contact with God.

Man has been made in God's class. Gen. 1:26-27, *"God said, 'Let us [Father, Son and Holy Spirit] make mankind in our image, after our likeness, and let them have complete authority over the fish of the sea, the birds of the air, the [tame] beasts, and over all of the earth, and over everything that creeps upon the earth.' So God created man in His own image, in the image and likeness of God He created him; male and female He created them."*1 God made man in such a way that we could fellowship with Him because we are a spirit even as He is a Spirit. John 4:24, *"God is a Spirit, and those who worship Him must worship Him in spirit and in truth."*

Since we are a spirit being we cannot touch the heart of God, who is a Spirit, physically or mentally, but must communicate with Him through our spirit man. It is only through spiritual communication that we can come to know God.

God manifested Himself physically when He took upon himself flesh (Jesus). John 1:1-3,14, *"In the beginning [before all time] was the Word (Christ), and the Word was with God, and the Word was God Himself. He was present originally with God. All things were made and came into existence through Him; and without Him was not even one thing made that has come into being". "And the Word (Christ) became flesh (human, incarnate) and tabernacled (fixed His tent of flesh, lived awhile) among us; and we [actually] saw His glory (His honor, His majesty), such glory as an only begotten Son receives from His Father, full of grace (favor, loving-kindness) and truth."*[1]

God was no less God when He took on flesh (Jesus), and man is no less man when he leaves his body at physical death. This is very evident in scripture when Jesus talks about Lazarus and the rich man at their deaths in Luke 16:19-31. The entire next chapter will be devoted to these verses.

SPIRITUAL DEATH

When we are physically born into this earth our spirits are alive unto God and we remain so until we are consciously aware of the rules set down by governing authorities whether it be God, parents, schools, etc. (laws). When we become conscious of these laws and break them we become spiritually dead (separated from God).

The Apostle Paul talks of this in Rom. 7:9, *"Once I was alive, but quite apart from and unconscious of the Law. But when the commandment came, sin lived again and I died (was sentenced by the Law to death)."*1 Once we are spiritually separated from God we no longer have a relationship with Him and, therefore, cannot fellowship with Him.

In order to be restored to God, man must then recognize that he is spiritually dead and needs to be born again. This was addressed by Jesus in John 3:3, 5-8. *"Most assuredly, I say to you, unless one is born again, he cannot see the Kingdom of God". "Unless one is born of water and the Spirit, he cannot enter the Kingdom of God. That which is born of flesh is flesh, and that which is born of the Spirit is spirit. Do not marvel that I said to you, 'You must be born again'. The wind blows where it wishes, and you hear the sound of it, but cannot tell where it comes from and where it goes. So is everyone who is born of the Spirit."*

This new birth experience brings us back into a right standing (righteousness) with God. We then have a Father-son/daughter relationship with Him in which we can then also fellowship with Him because our spirits are alive once more unto God. Rom. 10:4, *"For Christ is the end of the Law [the limit at which it ceases to be, for the law leads up to Him who is the fulfillment of its types, and in Him the purpose which it was designed to accomplish is fulfilled. That is, the purpose of the Law is fulfilled in Him] as the means of righteousness (right relationship to God) for everyone who trusts in and adheres to and relies on Him."*[1]

SPIRITUAL LIFE

You may be asking at this point, "How does a person become born again, or saved?" (These words mean the same thing). This is done very simply by asking Jesus Christ into your life as it states in Rom. 10:9-10,13 *"That if you confess with your mouth the Lord Jesus, and believe in your heart that God has raised Him from the dead, you will be saved. For with the heart one believes unto righteousness, and with the mouth confession is made unto salvation." "For whoever calls upon the name of the Lord shall be saved."*

Upon making this confession, your body and your mind do not change. If you are bald headed before the new birth, you will still bald headed afterward! However, there is an immediate change in your spirit man, the real you, the inner man. With that confession you receive a new nature, or, as the Bible states, you become a completely new creation. II Cor. 5:17, *"Therefore, if any person is [ingrafted] in Christ (the Messiah) he is a new creation (a new creature altogether);*

the old [previous moral and spiritual condition] has passed away. Behold, the fresh and new has come!"[1]

The real you, the spirit man, that new creation which is alive unto God, is what I have endeavored to emphasize because that is what life and death is all about. The Word of God has much to say about your human spirit, but I believe we have covered this sufficiently for you to see how it relates to physical and spiritual death.

It is the understanding of your spirit man and who you are in Christ Jesus, the awareness of your new relationship with God as your Father, which will free you fully and forever of any fear or uncertainty you may have ever had concerning death. Jesus said in John 3:15-16, *"In order that everyone who believes in Him [who cleaves to Him, trusts Him and relies on Him] may not perish, but have eternal life and [actually] live forever! For God so greatly loved and dearly prized the world that He [even] gave up His only begotten (unique) Son, so that whoever believes in (trusts in, clings to, relies on) Him shall not perish (come to destruction, be lost) but have eternal (everlasting) life."*[1]

Chapter 6

LAZARUS & THE RICH MAN

THE STORY OF LAZARUS and the rich man was mentioned in a previous chapter but discussion of the story was reserved for a chapter of its own because it has so much to tell us. You can readily see, from a study of these verses, that we (our spirit man and our souls) never lose a state of consciousness at the time of physical death.

It is important to note that these words are words spoken by Jesus Christ Himself, and that He starts out in Luke 16:19-31 by saying, *"There was a certain rich man..."* Dake's Annotated Reference Bible has this to say in the footnote to these scriptures:

"There was or there was not—which? If there was not, then Christ told an untruth, for He said there was. Even if this story was a parable, it is still true for it actually happened. Christ never did use lies to illustrate truths. But this is no parable any more than the previous verse, verse 18 ("whosoever put away his wife, and shall marry another, committeth adultery..."). In no parable of Christ is a person named, but certain points are always given which the parable illustrates. Here, there is no point illustrated.

The story is a literal one of two beggars: one begged in this life; the other begged in the next life. This shows plainly the conditions of departed souls between death and resurrection. It is satanic fallacy to make the story represent the Jews and Gentiles or portray any idea that is not stated in the text itself. The whole purpose of so doing on the part of false religionists is to do away with the reality of eternal hell and eternal punishment; or the reality of a temporary hell and torment.

It can be seen from the actual experience of these two men that Jesus Christ was declaring in plain terms the reality of the immortality of the soul, the consciousness of souls after leaving the body, the fact of different places for the righteous and the wicked between death and resurrection of the body, and the truth of torment for the wicked and bliss for the righteous."

Luke 16:19-31, *"There was a certain rich man, who was clothed in purple and fine linen, and fared sumptuously every day.*

But there was a certain beggar named Lazarus, full of sores, who was laid at his gate, desiring to be fed with the crumbs which fell from the rich man's table. Moreover the dogs came and licked his sores.

So it was that the beggar died, and was carried by the angels into Abraham's bosom. The rich man also died, and was buried.

And being in torments in Hades, he lifted up his eyes and saw Abraham afar off, and Lazarus in his bosom.

And he cried and said, 'Father Abraham, have mercy on me, and send Lazarus that he may dip the tip of his finger in water and cool my tongue; for I am tormented in this flame.'

But Abraham said, 'Son remember that in your lifetime you received your good things, and likewise Lazarus evil things; but now he is comforted, and you are tormented.

And besides all this, between us and you there is a great gulf fixed, so that those who want to pass from here to you cannot, nor can those from there pass to us. '

Then he said, 'I beg you therefore, father, that you would send him to my father's house,

For I have five brothers, that he may testify to them, lest they also come to this place of torment.'

Abraham said to him, 'They have Moses and the prophets; let them hear them.'

And he said, 'No, father Abraham; but if one goes unto them from the dead, they will repent.'

But he said to him, 'If they hear not Moses and the prophets, neither will they be persuaded though one rise from the dead.'"

RECOGNIZING THE DEPARTED

One of the questions I have heard asked most frequently concerning death is, "Will we know each other in the hereafter?" I think it should be obvious that we will be recognized by others just as Lazarus and the rich man recognized not only each other but Abraham as well. Another common expression is, "There is no such thing as hell, the only hell there is, is on this earth—when you die that's all there is." Again I say, it is obvious from what Jesus said that there is a grave and there is a hell.

I want to emphasize a point that was stated earlier, but which bears repeating here. ***Our believing or not believing something will not change that which is true!*** We are free moral agents with a God given ability to choose. In this case the choice is either eternal life or eternal death. The latter is *eternal separation* from God!

PARADISE

It is important, at this point to explain about paradise and Abraham's bosom. Abraham's bosom is a phrase used by the Jews to signify paradise. Paradise was located in the lower parts of the earth. There also is another paradise in the third heaven (Luke 23:43; II Cor. 12:1-4; Rev. 2:7). The Greek for paradise means a park, pleasure-grounds, forest or orchard and is used in the Septuagint (the most ancient Greek version of the Old Testament) for the Garden of Eden. Also, in

Hebrew, *paradise* is translated *orchard* or *forest*. Being in the bosom of another means the one next to him at that time, or of close relationship.2

Before the resurrection of Jesus Christ all the righteous spirits and souls, at the time of physical death, went to paradise and their bodies to the grave. When Christ died His body went to the grave, but He (spirit and soul) went to paradise and liberated those righteous dead (captives), taking them to heaven with Him when He ascended on high. Eph. 4:8-10 *"Therefore He says: 'When He ascended on high, He led captivity captive, and gave gifts to men'. (Now this, 'He ascended'—what does it mean but, that He also first descended into the lower parts of the earth? He who descended is also the one who ascended far above all the heavens, that He might fill all things)."* Then in Matt. 27:51-53 we see the evidence of those released who were held in paradise, following the resurrection of Jesus. *"Then, behold, the veil of the temple was torn in two from top to bottom; and the earth quaked and the rocks were split, and the graves were opened; and many bodies of the saints who had fallen asleep were raised; and coming out of the graves after His resurrection, they went into the Holy City and appeared to many."*

OUR RESURRECTION

Now when a Christian dies, he no longer is held captive in the lower parts of the earth, but he goes immediately to heaven to await the resurrection of the body. II Cor. 5:8, *"[Yes] we have confident and hopeful courage and are pleased rather to be away from home out of the body and be at home with the Lord."*[1] The Bible tells us that Christ now holds the keys to hell and death (Rev. 1:18).

Paradise under the earth has been emptied, but torment in Hades is being filled daily by the unsaved. It will continue to hold the wicked dead until after the Millennium, the one thousand year reign of Christ on this earth, which He will share with all those who have joined Him in heaven over the years. At that time Hades will deliver up the wicked dead to face judgment, at which time they will be cast, spirit, soul, and body, into eternal hell.

Rev. 20:12-15, *"And I saw the dead, small and great, stand before God; and the books were opened: and another book was opened, which is the book of life: and the dead were judged out of those things which were written in the books, according to their works. And the sea gave up the dead which were in it; and death and hell delivered up the dead which were in them: and they were judged every man according to their works. And death and hell were cast into the lake of fire. This is the second death. And whosoever was not found written in the book of life was cast into the lake of fire."*[2]

Now let's look closely at this story of the two men that died and contrast their conditions during their lives on earth and their departed life.

SEVEN FACTS ABOUT LAZARUS

1. He was a beggar full of sores which the dogs licked.

2. Laid at the rich man's gate to beg crumbs from his table.

3. Died and his body was buried.

4. His soul and spirit were carried to paradise by angels.

5. He was with Abraham and all the saints.

6. He was in comfort; no hell, no torment, no separation from the saved, no crying for mercy, no regrets of the past, and no thirst or punishment in hell-fire.

7. He retained spirit and soul faculties capable of enjoying eternity with God.

SEVEN FACTS ABOUT THE RICH MAN

1. Clothed in purple and fared sumptuously every day.

2. Died and his body was buried.

3. His spirit and soul went to hell.

4. He was in torment.

5. He had eyes that could see and recognize people.

6. He cried for mercy and begged for Lazarus to bring a drop of water to cool his tongue.

7. He still had a tongue, eyes, memory, intelligence, feelings, emotions, will, voice, reasoning powers, concern for his brothers, and all other soul passions and spirit faculties.

These scriptures clearly describe the actual experience of two beggars—one in this lifetime and one in the next. Their lives are contrasted before and after physical death. They tell of an impassable gulf between two abodes of the departed souls, the disillusionment of wicked and deceived unbelievers, and finally that the Word of God is the final authority and last court of appeal in determining our final destiny.[2]

Chapter 7

VICTORY OVER DEATH, HELL, & THE GRAVE

GOD IS THE AUTHOR OF LIFE and in Him there is no death. James 1:17, *"Every good gift and every perfect gift is from above, and comes down from the Father of lights, with whom there is no variation or shadow of turning."* Jesus said in John 10:10, *"The thief comes only in order to steal and kill and destroy. I came that they may have and enjoy life, and have it in abundance (to the full, till it overflows)."*1 Jesus tells us in this verse that it is the devil that steals, kills, and destroys, but that God through Jesus gives us the abundant life.

The power of Satan was destroyed, loosened, through the death, burial and resurrection of Jesus Christ. I John 3:8, *"For this purpose the Son of God was manifested, that He might destroy the works of the devil."* Throughout the scriptures, Old and New Testaments, God speaks to man telling him that He takes no pleasure in the death of any man, and that with long life will He show us His salvation. There are literally hundreds of scriptures that disclose and uphold God's intentions of giving us life as opposed to those of the devil (Satan) which are devised to steal, kill, and destroy us.

We hear people say, "I don't understand why God took So-and-So home!" First of all, God never takes anyone's life—to do so He would have to go against His own inherent nature, which is life. Secondly, at the time of physical death, God takes no one home to heaven, but rather receives them unto Himself.

ADAM'S SIN CAUSED SPIRITUAL & PHYSICAL DEATH

Every person that is born into the earth will eventually die physically, except those Christians (who have made Jesus Christ their Lord and Savior) who will be caught away to meet Jesus in the air. I Thess. 4:17, *"Then we who are alive and remain shall be caught up together with them in the clouds to meet the Lord in the air. And thus we shall always be with the Lord."*

Man was created to live eternally! Even after the sin of Adam passed on to all mankind, God made provision for all mankind to return to a state of being spiritually alive for all eternity. The first man, Adam, died spiritually before he died physically—he separated himself from God. Gen. 2:17, *"But of the tree of the knowledge of good and evil, you shall not eat, for in the day that you eat of it you shall surely die."* The literal Hebrew meaning of "you shall surely die", is "in dying (spiritually) you shall die (physically)." Adam lived physically for another 800 years after he died spiritually (became separated from God).

Because of Adam's sin, sin fell upon all mankind. But God's plan from the beginning was to redeem (buy back for the purpose of setting free) mankind, and He did it by becoming incarnate (flesh) through His Son Jesus Christ!

JESUS DESTROYED THE POWER OF DEATH

The Bible calls Jesus the last Adam, and it says that Jesus Christ tasted death for every man in order to deliver us from the fear of death. *"In as much then as the children have partaken of flesh and blood, He Himself likewise shared in the same, that through death He might destroy him who had the power of death, that is, the devil, and release those who through fear of death were all their lifetime subject to bondage."* (Heb. 2:14-15) Jesus destroyed (paralyzed) the power of death. We can pass from death to life (eternal) through salvation, being born again.

We talked about being born again in Chapter 5, and about how a person can receive eternal life, as stated in Rom. 10:9-10.

LIFE ETERNAL

As believers we will never see death because the moment we receive Jesus Christ as our personal Savior, we passed from death into life eternal! The "old man" died and now I have the life of God alive in my spirit man which is eternal. Because of Jesus' death, burial, and resurrection, death is a defeated enemy—death is abolished. We will never experience death—we just move from one space suit to another (leave our bodies).

In II Cor. 5:17 where we are called a new creation or new creatures, the correct literal translation actually means a new species of man, one who is alive forever-more!! The Apostle Paul talks about physical death as being a departure. II Tim. 4:6, *"For I am already being poured out as a drink offering, and the time of my departure is at hand"* Phil. 1:21-23, *"For me to live is Christ [His life in me], and to die is gain [the gain of the glory of eternity]. If, however, it is to be life in the flesh and I am to live on here, that means fruitful service for me; so I can say nothing as to my personal preference [I cannot choose], but I am hard pressed between the two. My yearning desire is to depart (to be free of this world, to set forth) and be with Christ, for that is far, far better."*1 Jesus, Himself, states in Rev. 1:18 that because of His death, burial, and resurrection, He is alive forevermore, and that He possesses the keys of death and hell. Because He accomplished this victory, the plan of salvation is made possible for all mankind.

SALVATION

Salvation is the major part of victory over death. The Greek word for salvation, "sozo", literally means preservation, soundness, wholeness, and healing. We have been given a gift for this life as well as the life to come. We pass from death to life through salvation— the "old man" died and we take the life of God within us. Gal. 2:20, *"I have been crucified with Christ [in Him I have shared His crucifixion]; it is no longer I who live, but Christ (the Messiah) lives in me; and the life I now live in the body I live by faith in (by adherence to and reliance on and complete trust in) the Son of God, who loved me and gave Himself up for me."*[1]

The Apostle Paul then goes on to say in Col. 3:1-4, *"If then you have been raised with Christ [to a new life, thus sharing His resurrection from the dead], aim at and seek the [rich, eternal treasures] that are above where Christ is, seated at the right hand of God. And set your minds and keep them set on what is above (the higher things), not on the things that are on the earth. For [as far as this world is concerned] you have died, and your [new, real] life is hidden with Christ in God. When Christ, who is our life, appears, then you will also appear with Him in [the splendor of His] glory."*[1] That which is born of God is eternal—overcomes death!

Jesus destroyed the power of death. My spirit is the life of my body and I walk in the spirit in this natural body which is subject to decay. Because my spirit is eternal, I will never have to experience death. You do not have to be sick to leave this physical natural world—you (your spirit) just leaves your body. God does not see death as we do. In fact, God never sees His children die because our spirits just enter into another realm (spiritual) which is more real than the one in which we now live.

Two examples of people's spirits leaving their bodies at death are recorded in Genesis. In Gen. 25:8, *"Then Abraham's spirit was released, and he died at a good (ample, full) old age, an old man, satisfied and satiated, and was gathered to his people."*[1] Gen. 35:29, *"And Isaac's spirit departed; he died and was gathered to his people, being an old man, satisfied and satiated with days; his sons Esau and Jacob buried him."*[1]

I could go on and on quoting scripture to show the departure of our spirits at the time of physical death, but it suffices to say that scripture does tell us of our departing spirits. The important thing to know is that death is the last enemy and that it is already put under our feet when we are released from the fear of physical death. The Bible tells the Christian that God did not give us a spirit of fear, but of power, and of love and of a sound mind (II Tim. 1:7).

JESUS IS OUR VICTORY

When we develop knowledge and understanding of God's Word concerning death, our faith increases and fear is replaced by that faith. It is through the scriptures that I have attempted to inform you of the truth concerning death. In I Cor. 15:47-57, the Spirit of God said through the Apostle Paul concerning death:

"The first man [was] from out of earth, made of dust (earthly-minded); the second Man [is] the Lord from out of heaven.

Now those who are made of the dust are like him who was first made of the dust (earthly-minded); and as is [the man] from heaven, so also [are those] who are of heaven (heavenly-minded).

And just as we have borne the image [of the man] of dust, so shall we and so let us also bear the image [of the Man] of heaven.

But I tell you this, brethren, flesh and blood cannot [become partakers of eternal salvation and] inherit or share in the kingdom of God; nor does the perishable (that which is decaying) inherit or share in the imperishable (the immortal).

Take notice! I tell you a mystery (a secret truth, an event decreed by the hidden purpose or counsel of God). We shall not all fall asleep [in death], but we shall all be changed (transformed) in a moment, in the twinkling of an eye, at the [sound of the] last trumpet call. For a trumpet will sound, and the dead [in Christ] will be raised imperishable (free and immune from decay), and we shall be changed (transformed).

For this perishable [part of us] must put on the imperishable [nature], and this mortal [part of us, this nature that is capable of dying] must put on immortality (freedom from death).

And when this perishable puts on the imperishable and this that was capable of dying puts on freedom from death, *then shall be fulfilled the scripture that says, death is swallowed up (utterly vanquished forever) in and unto victory.*

Oh death, where is your victory? Oh death, where is your sting?

Now sin is the sting of death, and sin exercises its power [upon the soul] through [the abuse of] the Law.

*But thanks be to God, Who gives us the victory [making us conquerors] through our Lord Jesus Christ."*1

COMFORTING & ENCOURAGING WORDS

Finally, in I Thess. 4:13-18, the Apostle Paul again addresses death with these comforting and encouraging words:

"Now also we would not have you ignorant, brethren, about those who fall asleep [in death], that you may not grieve [for them] as the rest do who have no hope [beyond the grave].

For since we believe that Jesus died and rose again, even so God will also bring with Him through Jesus those who have fallen asleep [in death].

For this we declare to you by the Lord's [own] word, that we who are alive and remain until the coming of the Lord shall in no way precede [into His presence] or have any advantage at all over those who have previously fallen asleep [in Him in death].

For the Lord Himself will descend from heaven with a loud cry of summons, with the shout of an archangel, and with the blast of the trumpet of God. And those who have departed this life in Christ will rise first.

Then we, the living ones who remain [on the earth], shall simultaneously be caught up along with [the resurrected dead] in the clouds to meet the Lord in the air; and so, always (through the eternity of eternities) we shall be with the Lord!

Therefore comfort and encourage one another with these words."[1]

HEAVEN IS A CHRISTIAN'S HOME

In Phil. 1:21-23 Paul said, *"For me to live is Christ, and to die is gain. But if I live on in the flesh, this will mean fruit from my labor; yet what I shall choose I cannot tell. For I am hard pressed between the two, having a desire to depart and be with Christ, which is far better."*

Most of us at some time or other have moved away from home. We've had to pull up our roots and leave the place that has been our shelter and our security all our lives. We can go to a place that we love and be with people we love and who love us. We can be happy, comfortable and secure in that new place and yet that particular home we left behind has a very special place deep down inside of us. In our hearts that's the place that will always be "home."

In the above verses what Paul is really saying is, "I love you, I'm happy with you, I rejoice with you, and you're part of my life; but I have deep in my heart that sense of being drawn toward, or belonging in, my heavenly home." You see, once we've made Jesus the Lord of our lives we become members of God's greater family, and our real home, our shelter and our security, is with God in heaven.

When we become born again, new creations in Christ (literally—a new species of man), as we seek God and study the Word, the inward man knows and grows stronger in the things of God. We no longer have the spirit of the world, but the Spirit of God alive on the inside of us (I Cor. 2:11-15). The outward man may be subject to frailty, but the inward man, the spirit man, the real us is renewed day by day, and when this body ceases to function, that inward man just moves home with God. In actuality we just depart from this bodily house to our home with God. God never sees His children die, He just welcomes us home. How many of us have children who live across the country and, oh, with what excitement and joy we eagerly prepare for their homecoming.

In I Peter 2:9-11 the Apostle Peter calls us aliens and strangers in this world. We're God's chosen people, called from the darkness of this world. And when we leave this natural earthly realm, God receives and welcomes us home as dearly loved children. While we're here on the earth, we're really away from home.

The Apostle Paul says that while we're at home here we are away from the Lord and that it is preferable to be absent from the body and at home with the Lord (II Cor. 5:6-8).

We saw in the previous text, Phil. 1:21-23, that it is *far* better to be with Christ—not good, nor better, but **far** better. If we know this, we can eagerly await our heavenly citizenship—we can look forward to going home to the Lord. Our inferior earthly bodies will be transformed into glorious immortal bodies (Phil. 3:20-21). We have total assurance that God has prepared for us—He's ready to receive us to Himself. When a Christian leaves this earthly body he has a home in glory, fully prepared for him by God Himself.

Those of us who remain surely do miss the presence of those we love, and certainly things cannot be the same for us without them. But oh, let your heart rejoice, sing and be glad, for the splendor in which our departed loved ones, and eventually we ourselves, will dwell with the Father. For those who know God, those who believe and trust Jesus Christ His resurrected Son as their Lord and Savior, the grave changes from a place of sorrow and mourning into a doorway which enters into that place of eternal joy and glory where we will all be united once again.

To get a Biblical perspective of heaven, you need to read the book of Revelation, chapters 21 and 22.

PRAYER OF COMMITMENT

JESUS SAID IN JOHN 14:2-3, *"In my Father's house are many mansions, if it were not so, I would have told you. I go to prepare a place for you. And if I go and prepare a place for you, I will come again and receive you unto myself; that where I am, there you may be also."* Jesus was talking about a Christian's heavenly abode.

Heb. 12:1, *"Therefore we also, since we are surrounded by so great a cloud of witnesses..."* Among this cloud of witnesses in heaven are those we know and love who had confessed Jesus Christ as Savior of their lives while they lived on this earth. Because you believe in and confess Jesus as your Lord and Savior, you will never have to say "I hope" I will go to heaven. You can know that you will.

If you are one of those who doesn't really know that you would go to heaven if you died today, and you desire assurance of a heavenly home, then turn your heart toward God, your Heavenly Father, and say this prayer unto eternal salvation.

PRAYER OF SALVATION

Heavenly Father, in the name of Jesus Christ, I present myself to You. I pray and ask Jesus to be Lord over my life. I believe in my heart, so I say with my mouth, that Jesus is Your own precious Son, and that He died and You raised

Him from the dead on my behalf. At this moment, I make Him my Savior and the Lord of my life. Jesus, come into my heart. I believe this moment that I am saved. I say now that I am born again; I am a Christian; I am now a child of Almighty God.

Now just thank God for making you His child and giving you eternal life, as you just inherited the Kingdom of God and the Kingdom of heaven. God bless you!

I take God the Father to be my Lord.

I take God the Son to be my Savior.

I take the Holy Spirit to be my Sanctifier.

I take the Word of God to be the rule of my life.

I take the people of God to be my people.

And I now commit myself—spirit, soul, and body—to my Lord and Savior Jesus Christ.

And I do this freely, fully, and forever.

In the Name of the Father, and the Son, and of the Holy Spirit. Amen.

REFERENCES

1. *The Amplified New Testament*, Copyright 1954, 1958, 1987 by the Lockman Foundation, LaHarra, CA, used by permission.

2. *Dake's Annotated Reference Bible*, King James Version (KJV), Copyright 1963, by Finis Jennings Dake, Lawrenceville, Georgia. Used by permission.

3. *Expository Dictionary of New Testament Words*, by W. E. Vine, M.A. Seventeenth Impression 1966, by the Fleming H. Rewell Co., Old Tappan, New Jersey.

AUTHOR CONTACT
INFORMATION

Chuck welcomes the opportunity to minister to your church, in conferences, or in men's, women's, or youth groups.

Additional copies of *Beyond the Horizon* are available from your local bookstore or online.

Charles G. Branz
Freedom, PA 15042
cg.branz@ymail.com